COURTING HISTORY

School Desegregation

Brown v. Board of Education of Topeka

BUDD BAILEY

Cavendish Square
New York

Published in 2019 by Cavendish Square Publishing, LLC
243 5th Avenue, Suite 136, New York, NY 10016

First Edition

Library of Congress Cataloging-in-Publication Data

Names: Bailey, Budd, 1955-, author.
Title: School desegregation : Brown v. Board of Education of Topeka / Budd Bailey.
Description: New York : Cavendish Square, 2018. | Series: Courting history |
Includes bibliographical references and index.
Identifiers: LCCN 2018003320 (print) | LCCN 2018005840 (ebook) |
ISBN 9781502639516 (eBook) | ISBN 9781502639530 (library bound) |
ISBN 9781502639523 (pbk.)
Subjects: LCSH: Brown, Oliver, 1918-1961--Trials, litigation, etc.--Juvenile literature. |
Topeka (Kan.). Board of Education--Trials, litigation, etc.--Juvenile literature. |
Segregation in education--Law and legislation--United States--Juvenile literature. |
African Americans--Civil rights--Juvenile literature.
Classification: LCC KF228.B76 (ebook) | LCC KF228.B76 B35 2018 (print) |
DDC 344.73/0798--dc23
LC record available at https://lccn.loc.gov/2018003320

Editorial Director: David McNamara
Editor: Chet'la Sebree
Copy Editor: Nathan Heidelberger
Associate Art Director: Amy Greenan
Designer: Joe Parenteau
Production Coordinator: Karol Szymczuk
Photo Research: J8 Media

The photographs in this book are used by permission and through the courtesy of: Cover, p. 5, 18 Carl Iwasaki/The LIFE Images Collection/Getty Images; p. 6 Wikimedia Commons/File:Dred Scott photograph (circa 1857).jpg/Public Domain; p. 7, 20, 22, 27, 32, 43, 44, 46, 48 Bettmann/Getty Images; p. 8 Universal History Archive/UIG/Getty Images; p. 13 Cornell Capa/The LIFE Picture Collection/Getty Images; p. 16 Jerry Engel/New York Post Archives /(c) NYP Holdings, Inc./ Getty Images; p. 17 Pierre Rochon/Alamy Stock Photo; p. 21 Hulton Archive/Getty Images; p. 24 AP Images; p. 25 Joseph Scherschel/The LIFE Picture Collection/Getty Images; p. 33 MPI/Getty Images; p. 34 Oscar White/Corbis/ VCG/Getty Images; p. 35 Peter Stackpole/The LIFE Picture Collection/Getty Images; p. 36 Library of Congress/Corbis/ Getty Images; p. 37 George Tames/New York Times Co./Getty Images; p. 42 Universal History Archive/Getty Images.

Printed in the United States of America

Contents

ONE

A Century of Segregation

It's the early 1950s in Topeka, Kansas. Two sisters are walking to elementary school on a fine autumn morning.

Linda Brown is the older of the two. She is probably looking out for her little sister Terry as they make their way to the school grounds. There is a school only seven blocks away from the family's house, but they are not allowed to go there. That school is for white children only. Linda and Terry are African American.

They head to another school for only African Americans in another part of town. To get there, the two schoolchildren have to walk six blocks and cross over some railroad tracks to catch a bus. The train tracks are busy, so this is dangerous.

Once Linda and Terry make it safely across, they wait to ride on a bus for 1 mile (1.6 kilometers) to their final destination. The one-way trip takes them more than ninety minutes. They make this trip day after day, year after year, because of the color of their skin.

In the 1950s, Topeka's schools were segregated, or divided, based on race. For that reason, the girls could not attend the all-white school close to home. In 1942, the city's school superintendent, Dr. Kenneth McFarland, said, "Segregated schools are here to stay."

A long walk to school for a couple of young sisters, Linda (*left*) and Terry (*right*), led their parents, Leola and Oliver, to get involved in one of the most famous legal cases in US history.

Leola and Oliver Brown, the parents of Linda and Terry, thought their daughters were receiving a good education. Even still, they did not think segregation was right. For that reason, they agreed to take part in a lawsuit against segregated schools. Four years later, a decision was handed down by the Supreme Court of the United States that changed the nation forever.

Slavery and Citizenship

The education of African Americans had been an issue throughout American history. The North and South had different systems in the first ninety years of the United States' existence. In the South, slavery was legal until 1865. At that time, it was illegal in some places to educate any black person, though a small percentage of African Americans did learn how to read and write. In the North, where slavery was mostly outlawed by the early 1800s, African Americans had better access to education.

If African Americans in the South had hopes of gaining equal rights as citizens before the Civil War, those hopes were dashed by the 1857 *Dred Scott* decision. Scott, an enslaved black man, had been brought to Illinois, a Free State, by his owner. Eventually, he tried to sue for his freedom.

Dred Scott tried to sue for his freedom, but he lost when the US Supreme Court ruled against him.

Scott won the initial court decision in *Scott v. Emerson*, but lost twice on appeal. An appeal is when a person who loses a court case asks a higher court to overturn a lower court's decision. After losing two appeals, Scott asked the US Supreme Court to review his case. Five of the nine Supreme Court justices were from families that owned slaves. Chief Justice Roger Taney, a supporter of slavery, and the court ruled that African Americans were not citizens of the United States in *Dred Scott v. Sandford*. For that reason, Scott did not have the right to sue for his freedom.

The Civil War began in 1861. It ended with a victory by the North in 1865. Within five years, the Constitution was amended to ban slavery and to give African Americans full rights as citizens of the United States. Despite this change in laws, it would take many years for the people to treat African Americans like citizens.

Segregation and Its Effects

In 1870, Senator Charles Sumner of Massachusetts, a leading advocate for equal rights, proposed a law. It would outlaw discrimination in juries, schools, transportation, and public accommodations, or any facility used by the public. As the bill went through the legislative process, the portions concerning eliminating school discrimination were dropped.

Senator Sumner attempted to change segregation laws with the Civil Rights Act of 1875.

The bill, eventually called the Civil Rights Act of 1875, was signed into law by President Ulysses S. Grant. However, the new law only lasted eight years. In 1883, the Supreme Court ruled that the act was unconstitutional (*Civil Rights Cases*). The court believed the Fourteenth Amendment, which had taken effect in 1868, did not outlaw discrimination by individuals or private businesses. It only outlawed discrimination by states. Therefore, it was legal to discriminate and segregate things like public accommodations.

One of the most famous court cases involving civil rights in US history challenged this idea. In 1890, Louisiana passed a law that required trains to have separate cars for white and black passengers. Two years later, Homer Plessy, who was seven-eighths white but still considered African American by Louisiana law, deliberately sat in the white car. He wanted to test the state's law. Plessy was arrested by authorities.

Justice Harlan disagreed with the rest of the Supreme Court in the *Plessy v. Ferguson* case.

In Plessy's first hearing, the court ruled against him. Judge John Howard Ferguson fined Plessy twenty-five dollars. Plessy and his lawyers appealed. The case climbed the legal ladder as Plessy's lawyers continued to appeal decisions against him. In 1896, the US Supreme Court agreed to hear the case.

The *Plessy v. Ferguson* ruling went against Plessy by a vote of 7–1. Justice Henry Billings Brown wrote the majority opinion, or written statement explaining the court's decision. He said that separate train cars did not violate the Fourteenth Amendment as long as they were equal. The phrase "separate but equal" has been used to describe this decision. Justice Brown's logic was that while the Fourteenth Amendment did affect the actions of the federal government, it did not apply to private individuals or businesses.

Justice John Marshall Harlan wrote a dissenting opinion, or a written statement that disagrees with the majority's decision. He wrote, "Our Constitution is color-blind and neither knows nor tolerates classes among citizens." In other words, he thought separating people because of their races went against the US Constitution.

Southern and border states, or states that allowed slavery but did not try to leave the Union before the Civil War, were quick to respond to the ruling. Many states' representatives were happy to set up separate facilities for the two races. These officials were also the ones who defined what "equal" would look like. Rarely were facilities designed for African Americans truly equal to the ones for white Americans.

These states passed a series of Jim Crow laws. These laws were designed to keep the races segregated. For instance, Missouri passed a law in 1929 that mandated separate schools for "children of African descent." The law made it "unlawful for any colored child to attend any white school, or any white child to attend a colored school." Similarly, many states forced black people and white people to use separate parks and bathrooms. Drinking fountains were marked "white" or "colored," a term for African Americans that is now viewed as offensive in the United States. In North Carolina, black and white students weren't allowed to use the same textbooks. In Florida, textbooks used by each race could not be stored in the same place. These types of policies continued for more than fifty years.

Around the Nation

Education decisions during much of US history have been left to states and cities. The federal government has rarely taken a large role. The first public high school in the United States, Boston English, opened in 1821 in Massachusetts. That state soon opened public schools to everyone. However, at the same time, it was illegal in most places to teach enslaved African Americans to read.

Things began to change during the Reconstruction Era (1865–1877), which immediately followed the Civil War. During this time, the North tried to change the laws and culture of the South. For instance, state constitutions in the South were rewritten to guarantee African Americans a free education. However, when federal troops left the region in 1877, many state officials rewrote these constitutions with Jim Crow policies. Those laws were later reinforced by the *Plessy v. Ferguson* decision. It took little time for Southern states to segregate schools.

African Americans were happy to receive any education at that point. However, they suffered in several ways. African Americans often had to deal with poor facilities, fewer and older textbooks, and teachers who did not receive the same pay as their white counterparts. Little changed during the next seventy-five years.

The Supreme Court does not easily reverse a previously made decision. In the years following *Plessy v. Ferguson*, other cases came up that seemed to expand on that original ruling. In 1899, the court ruled that a tax could be placed on black and white community members to pay for the construction of a new school, even if only white students could attend it. In 1908, Berea College in Kentucky was ordered by the Supreme Court to segregate its students.

However, World War II changed some attitudes. African Americans fought for the United States, returned home, and continued to be treated as second-class citizens. President Harry Truman recognized this issue. He asked Congress to improve the rights of African Americans. Ultimately, he desegregated the armed forces in 1948. This meant that white and black Americans could fight side by side in the same unit. In general, however, progress related to desegregation and equal rights was slow.

Would those new attitudes be enough to overturn *Plessy v. Ferguson* and desegregate schools? African Americans were ready to find out.

TWO

Step by Step

Thurgood Marshall was a lawyer for the National Association for the Advancement of Colored People (NAACP), an organization dedicated to equality and the end of race-based discrimination. In the early 1950s, he had a significant victory in the battle to desegregate educational institutions. The case was called *Sweatt v. Painter*.

In 1946, Heman Sweatt, a black man, had applied to the University of Texas law school. He was turned down because of his race. The school said that Sweatt was welcome to study at the university's law school for African Americans. It was opening in 1947. Marshall and the NAACP sued. In the courtroom, Marshall and fellow attorney Robert Carter argued that the new law school clearly did not have equal facilities, including the library, course offerings, and teachers. These unequal options violated the equal protection clause in the Fourteenth Amendment to the Constitution. It also did not meet the "separate but equal" standard of *Plessy v. Ferguson*.

The US Supreme Court agreed with Marshall, unanimously. However, it did not take the added step of throwing out *Plessy v. Ferguson*'s precedent, or legal standard. In the fifty-four years since that decision, the court obviously

Thurgood Marshall was a tireless advocate for desegregating public schools. The attorney for the NAACP worked on many key cases regarding discrimination and equal rights for African Americans.

had changed some—but not all—of its views on segregation. The *Sweatt v. Painter* ruling gave Marshall some hope that the court would be willing to desegregate public schools.

Brown v. Board of Education of Topeka

The next step for the NAACP would be to find situations around the country that could serve as test cases, or legal actions designed to set new precedents. The Brown family's situation proved to be a good fit. Oliver Brown filed a lawsuit in a local district court on February 28, 1951, along with twelve other parents affected by segregation in Topeka. All of those parents had tried to enroll their children in the all-white school that was closest to their homes. The target of the suit was the Topeka School Board. One of the parents' major arguments was that the all-black school would not be able to provide as good of an educational experience as one provided by a fully integrated, or desegregated, school.

Dr. Hugh Speer, chairman of the University of Missouri-Kansas City's Department of Education, agreed. In his court testimony, or sworn legal statement, he said:

> If the colored children are denied the experience in school of associating with white children, who represent 90 percent of our national society in which these colored children must live, then the colored child's curriculum is being greatly curtailed. The Topeka curriculum or any school curriculum cannot be equal under segregation.

In other words, Dr. Speer believed that African American children would benefit from attending school with white children since most of the United States was made up of white Americans. He also did not believe that any school could be both separate and equal.

The school board responded by saying that some African Americans had thrived under the "separate but equal" system. The board listed men like George Washington Carver, a botanist and inventor, and Booker T. Washington, an educator and writer.

The district court sided with the school district. The main reason was that the *Plessy v. Ferguson* decision was still the legal precedent on the issue of segregation. It was a decision made by the US Supreme Court, the country's highest court. District courts are the lowest court in the federal court system. The local judges did not feel they had the authority to overturn a Supreme Court ruling.

The three judges on the district court, however, did not necessarily feel good about ruling in favor of the school board. They wrote in the decision that segregated schools had negative effects on their students:

> The impact is greater when it has the sanction of the law; for the policy of separating the races is usually interpreted as denoting the inferiority of the Negro group. A sense of inferiority affects the motivation of a child to learn. Segregation with the sanction of law, therefore, has a tendency to [slow] the educational and mental development of Negro children and to deprive them of some of the benefits they would receive in a racial[ly] integrated school system.

In other words, the judges thought the law would make African American children feel inferior. The judges believed that making African American children feel inferior would make them feel less motivated to learn.

Other Test Cases

The other test cases brought by the NAACP had similar themes to the one in Kansas. In South Carolina, Harry Briggs joined nineteen parents in suing the head of the Clarendon County School Board, R. W. Elliott. In *Briggs v. Elliott*, the parents pointed out that bus transportation was provided for white students but not for black ones. The parents' petition to change that situation had been ignored. In this case, Marshall pointed out that segregated schools branded African American children as inferior. The US district court in South Carolina voted 2–1 against the parents. However, the court did order the school board to make the schools more equal.

From left: Harry Briggs Jr., Linda Brown Smith, Spottswood Bolling Jr., and Ethel Louise Belton Brown. As children, they were all part of the combined *Brown v. Board of Education* case. They are shown here in 1964, ten years after the decision.

Delaware had two such cases: *Belton v. Gebhart* and *Bulah v. Gebhart*. Both dealt with transportation issues. In the *Belton* case, African American children had to go 20 miles (32 km) in the Wilmington area for school. In the *Bulah* case, Sarah Bulah had to drive her daughter 2 miles (3.2 km) to a one-room schoolhouse. African American children did not receive bus transportation to school. However, a bus for white schoolchildren went by Bulah's house two times per day.

Judge Collin Seitz ruled in favor of Belton and Bulah in a combined case. He ordered the schools to admit the black students into the all-white schools. He said the situation had been a violation of the "separate but equal" policy. However, the ruling only applied to the two school districts in question. It did not change policy throughout the state.

In Virginia, Barbara Johns led a large student protest when the Prince Edward County School Board failed to build a new school for African Americans. The NAACP took on the case, and parents in the district sued to end desegregation. A US district court ruled in favor of the school board (*Davis v. County School Board of Prince Edward County*).

Finally, in the District of Columbia, several black parents tried to enroll their children into John Philip Sousa Junior High School. Their request was denied. Again, parents sued the school board, and again a district court ruled in favor of the schools (*Bolling v. Sharpe*).

The Capitol Square Civil Rights Memorial in Richmond, Virginia, honors Barbara Johns for leading a student protest.

Most of these cases ruled against the African American plaintiffs, or the people that bring a case to court. Many of these cases used *Plessy v. Ferguson* as legal precedent for the decision. There was a growing feeling, however, that there was a big problem with the national educational system. There was only one real way to change it.

The Road to the Supreme Court

Sometimes legal cases can wind their way through the various levels of our court system for years, but this matter was different. It was obvious that the Supreme Court would be the only judicial group that could write a definitive decision on the matter. Would it do so? The Supreme Court turns down the chance to rule on the majority of the cases that it is asked to review. Since *Plessy v. Ferguson* was still the legal standard in cases about segregation, the court could simply walk away from the entire matter without comment.

Some of the children and parents who were part of the *Brown v. Board of Education* case gathered in 1953 for this group photograph.

The issue generated plenty of debate among the justices of the Supreme Court. Eventually, they announced that the court would hear arguments on the matter. That itself was a huge win for the plaintiffs. The five test cases (counting Delaware's two similar suits as one) were combined. The case would use Oliver Brown's name since his came first in the listing of all of the cases in the dispute. The case and the landmark decision the justices made would forever be known as *Brown v. Board of Education of Topeka*.

The Other Branches

In the United States federal government, the judicial branch of government is an equal partner with the executive and legislative branches. In the early half of the twentieth century, opinions about civil rights differed among them.

The State Department, the section of the executive branch responsible for overseeing US relations with other countries, might have been the biggest supporter of civil rights in the executive branch. It thought the end of school segregation would help relations with foreign countries during the Cold War, a tense period between the United States and the Soviet Union. However, President Dwight Eisenhower was cautious about the federal government's attempts to improve civil rights. He thought it would be best if changes started on the local level.

Meanwhile, in Congress, representatives from Southern states posed the greatest resistance to laws focused on civil rights. They often had a great deal of seniority, or high rankings. They used this seniority to block proposed laws related to civil rights. Senator Richard Russell of Georgia strongly believed African Americans were inferior. He frequently blocked any civil rights legislation through the use of the filibuster, or an attempt to delay or stop the approval of a piece of proposed legislation.

In theory, both branches could have acted to try to end school segregation. They did not.

THREE

The Two Arguments

The Supreme Court has an impressive home. The four-story building has marble steps and eight large columns that give it a sense of importance. The 252-foot (77-meter) plaza in front of the building is familiar to many as the setting for media interviews as well as public demonstrations concerning important cases.

Hundreds of people lined up for the chance to hear the arguments in the *Brown v. Board of Education* case.

Sometimes the affairs of the court can go unnoticed. However, December 9, 1952, was a big day. This was the day that arguments would begin for *Brown v. Board of Education of Topeka*. The nation watched with great anticipation.

When attorney Robert Carter first started to speak to the nine justices of the Supreme Court, the clock read 1:35 p.m. Every seat in the courtroom was taken. About three hundred people were there to watch. About half of them were African Americans. Another five hundred people waited in line without getting the chance to sit and watch. Reporters for media outlets were there. They shared news of the case with the rest of the nation and the world.

Robert Carter played an important role in the NAACP's legal case against segregated schools.

Some of those people might have looked at the entrance to the building on their way in. On the building, they would have seen the words "Equal Justice Under Law." But what did that mean? Historian Richard Kluger asks, "Could 'Equal Justice' truly be read to mean 'Separate but Equal Justice'?" The process to find out was about to begin.

Shifting Tides

America had been waiting for this moment for years. In the first few decades after the *Plessy v. Ferguson* decision, rules about the legality of school segregation had expanded.

However, in the two decades or so before the *Brown v. Board of Education* hearing, the legal momentum had started to shift in the other direction. A series of decisions had chipped away at the idea of "separate but equal."

Some of those decisions took place after Franklin Roosevelt became president in 1933. This probably was not a coincidence. Roosevelt believed that the federal government should take an active role in the lives of American citizens. This philosophy was one of the guiding principles behind the New Deal. That was the name for the series of programs Roosevelt launched to pull the United States out of the Great Depression in the 1930s.

President Franklin Roosevelt tried to change some segregation laws in the United States but found that progress was slow.

However, the Supreme Court is slower to change course than the other branches of government. This is because of the lack of turnover in its members. The nine justices are appointed for life.

Several laws featuring large policy changes were signed by Roosevelt in the 1930s. They sometimes were ruled unconstitutional by the court. Roosevelt, however, stayed in office long enough to see the court change. He eventually appointed new justices. Their beliefs were closer to Roosevelt's than the old justices' beliefs were. The new justices often voted to uphold the president's actions.

One of the first changes to segregation laws came in 1936. It involved a state court and not the US Supreme Court. A black student in Maryland wanted to attend law school in that state. However, there was no law school for African Americans there. He sued in the case known as *Murray v. Pearson*.

The university cited *Plessy v. Ferguson* as its reason for not admitting Donald Murray. His rejection letter read, "The University of Maryland does not admit Negro students, and your application is accordingly rejected." However, the University of Maryland was the only such law school in the state. For that reason, the university was ordered to admit Murray. Thurgood Marshall argued the case on Murray's behalf. It was one of Marshall's earliest courtroom victories.

A similar case came up in 1938, when Lloyd Gaines wanted to be admitted to the University of Missouri's law school. It was an all-white institution. He was turned down because of his race even though there was no law school for black students. The US Supreme Court ruled in a 7–2 vote that Gaines's Fourteenth Amendment rights had been violated. The case was called *Missouri ex rel. Gaines v. Canada*.

Lloyd Gaines mysteriously disappeared after winning a legal case that would have allowed him to attend an all-white law school.

Unfortunately, Gaines disappeared after the decision. A family member believed Gaines had been murdered.

More cases followed. A federal appeals court ruled segregated schooling for Mexican Americans in California was illegal in 1947. A year later, the Supreme Court ruled a black student had to be admitted to the University of Oklahoma's law school because there was no equivalent school for African Americans.

Finally, the Supreme Court ruled against discrimination in two cases in 1950. One stopped an attempt by the University of Oklahoma to isolate a black graduate student from his white classmates. The other was the previously mentioned

Through *Sweatt v. Painter*, Heman Sweatt achieved his goal of attending law school at the University of Texas.

Sweatt v. Painter case, which ordered the University of Texas to admit a black applicant to its law school.

The Case Before the Court

While the spectators in the court chamber that day in 1952 may not have known about those cases, the two sides of *Brown v. Board of Education* knew them well. The Supreme Court justices were familiar with them too.

During the hearing, the court went through the five cases that had been combined into *Brown*. They discussed the slightly different circumstances of each case. For example, the *Bolling v. Sharpe* case was centered in the District of Columbia.

DC residents have a different legal status than people who live in states. They do not have direct representation in Congress and could not vote in presidential elections at the time.

The Case for the Plaintiffs

After going over the background of the cases, it was time to hear the arguments of the plaintiffs and the defendants. The plaintiffs consisted of black students and their parents. They were represented by the legal department of the NAACP. Their main argument was that segregated schools violated students' Fourteenth Amendment rights.

Section 1 of the Fourteenth Amendment to the Constitution says:

> No State shall make or enforce any law which shall abridge the privileges or immunities of citizens of the United States; nor shall any State deprive any person of life, liberty, or property, without due process of law; nor deny to any person within its jurisdiction the equal protection of the laws.

In other words, no state shall have laws that take away or reduce the rights of US citizens. Additionally, no state shall create laws that treat citizens differently. All citizens have the right to be treated the same as other citizens by the law.

That last part is crucial. African Americans were not being treated equally in the area of education. They were being forced to attend segregated schools that were often considered inferior to their white counterparts.

Since the District of Columbia was not part of a state, it could be argued that the Fourteenth Amendment did not apply to its policies concerning school segregation. However,

NACCP lawyer James Nabrit used the Fifth Amendment to the Constitution in his verbal argument. That amendment says that "No person shall be … deprived of life, liberty, or property, without due process of law." In other words, all citizens are deserving of the right to be treated fairly by the law. Nabrit believed that there was no legal basis for excluding a student based on race in DC.

The Case for the Defense

The lawyers for the defendants of the case took an opposite approach. The Supreme Court had ruled in 1896 that segregation was allowed in the United States as long as there were separate but equal facilities for the two races.

John Davis and Thurgood Marshall talk during a break in the *Brown v. Board of Education* case.

Thurgood Marshall

Thurgood Marshall, a Baltimore native, was a standout in academics. In 1933, he graduated first in his class from Howard University School of Law in Washington, DC. Marshall briefly had his own law practice, but then he joined the NAACP in 1936. The *Brown* case turned him into one of the most prominent lawyers in the nation.

Marshall's career shifted gears when President John Kennedy appointed him as a judge for the US Court of Appeals for the Second Circuit in 1961. In 1965, President Lyndon Johnson named Marshall the solicitor general, the person who supervises and conducts government legal actions in the United States Supreme Court.

Johnson then picked him in 1967 for his greatest honor: associate justice of the United States Supreme Court. Marshall was the first African American Supreme Court justice. He stayed on the court through 1991.

Marshall believed that "the legal system can force open doors and sometimes even knock down walls, but it cannot build bridges ... We will only attain freedom if we learn to appreciate what is different and muster the courage to discover what is fundamentally the same." In other words, he thought that the law was just the first step in a fully integrated society. He thought people must acknowledge their differences while also being brave enough to see their similarities.

John Davis was one of the lawyers for the defendants in South Carolina's *Briggs v. Elliott* case. He therefore served as one of the defense lawyers in the combined *Brown v. Board of Education* case. He believed that there was "no reason assigned here why this Court or any other should reverse the findings" of *Plessy v. Ferguson*. In other words, the case essentially had been decided by the Supreme Court more than fifty years before the current hearing.

Davis also had an opinion about fully integrating all US public schools. He did not believe that recent court cases meant that a bigger policy needed to be changed. He believed those cases were "decided solely on the basis of inequality." That meant they did not follow the "separate but equal" guidelines of *Plessy v. Ferguson*. He did not think those cases meant the whole policy needed to be changed. Rather, the cases demonstrated the need to follow the policy.

The defense team also offered a different argument about how the Fourteenth Amendment should be applied to *Brown v. Board of Education*. They said that equal treatment under the law did not mean the exact same treatment. The defendants thought children should be taught in the most comfortable learning environment possible. That could mean white children should be grouped with other white children, while black children shared a classroom with other black children.

Back and Forth Arguments

The arguments went back and forth during three days of testimony. The defendants said that the United States government usually left decisions about education to the states and cities. Therefore, it would be a big jump to allow the federal government to make a decision in the matter of segregation now. In addition, there was little public education when the Fourteenth Amendment was created. Did it apply to the system used more than eighty years after it became law?

The plaintiffs used a similar argument about the lack of public education in the nineteenth century. No one could be sure what the Supreme Court had in mind when it came to segregation in education in 1896. Also, the *Plessy v. Ferguson* case was about railroad transportation. Attaching the ruling to a law about education might be incorrect.

Psychologists testified that black children suffered because of school segregation, as they had a lower self-image than their white counterparts. The Topeka school board answered that no such studies had been done on its students, so no specific damage could be shown.

H. Albert Young, the attorney general of Delaware, said that the state planned to build better schools for African Americans. NAACP co-counsels Louis Redding and Jack Greenberg answered by saying black students still would have to be bused a long distance under that plan.

By the end of the last session, momentum seemed to be on the side of those suing to end school segregation. However, anything seemed possible.

Reverend Joseph DeLaine was an African American leader in South Carolina. He attended the oral arguments. Afterwards, he said he had watched all of the justices in an attempt to guess their reactions to the arguments. He especially watched Chief Justice Fred Vinson. The chief justice is the court's main judge. "I was afraid of Vinson's face," Reverend DeLaine said.

FOUR

A Ruling in Two Parts

A subject as explosive as school segregation already had plenty of drama associated with it when the Supreme Court discussed it in 1952. The *Brown v. Board of Education* case would add to that level of drama in the next few years as it became one of the most famous cases in American history.

As a general rule, the Supreme Court justices meet to discuss a case shortly after the case's hearing. Under normal circumstances, the chief justice will ask the associate justices their views on the matter. If positions are firm and one side has a clear majority, the chief justice will assign himself or another justice the task of writing the majority opinion, or a written statement about the court's decision. The other justices are given the chance to add their own written opinions in agreement or opposition to the decision.

The nine justices reviewed the *Brown* case thoroughly. However, they never got around to voting, which is unusual. All of the justices took notes on the discussion, and scholars have been allowed to examine those documents. From those documents, it looks like four of the justices—Hugo Black, William O. Douglas, Harold Burton, and Sherman Minton—were ready to throw out the "separate but equal" ruling of *Plessy v. Ferguson*. Chief Justice Frederick Vinson

George E. C. Hayes (*left*), Thurgood Marshall (*center*), and James Nabrit Jr. (*right*) celebrate their legal victory in the *Brown v. Board of Education* case.

and Justice Thomas Clark wondered about the uproar a desegregation order might cause. It looked like Justice Stanley Reed would uphold the *Plessy v. Ferguson* precedent. The other two justices—Felix Frankfurter and Robert Jackson—weren't sure what to do. Jackson did not like overturning precedent but was willing to join the majority in overturning *Plessy v. Ferguson.*

Frankfurter might have been the most torn over the issue. He was a consistent opponent of segregation throughout the country. However, he had problems with the judicial branch taking a step that would change American society in a dramatic way. Frankfurter also wondered how the country would respond to a divided decision. Would the South revolt?

He thought agreement among the justices would give a decision more weight.

Some scholars believe that if the justices had to take an actual vote, they would have upheld the *Plessy* precedent 5–4. However, there are others who have looked at the same material and guessed that school segregation would have been banned by a 5–4 vote.

Justice Frankfurter had mixed feelings about how the *Brown* case should be decided.

What did Frankfurter do under the circumstances? He stalled. The associate justice asked to have the two sides come back at a future time to reargue the case. The rest of the court went along with the idea. Frankfurter sent questions about the Fourteenth Amendment to the parties involved in the case. Specifically, he asked what effect school desegregation would have on the country.

And then, an event unexpectedly changed the course of American history. Chief Justice Vinson died.

Chief Justice Frederick Vinson

Vinson had a fascinating career in public service. The Kentucky native graduated from Normal School in Kentucky and studied law at Centre College Law. While there, he had the highest grades in the history of the school. After working as an attorney for the state of Kentucky, Vinson was elected to the House of Representatives in 1924. He became friends with Harry Truman of Missouri.

The death of Chief Justice Frederick Vinson may have changed American history.

Vinson left Congress to become a judge on the United States Court of Appeals for the District of Columbia Circuit. During World War II, he worked as director of the Office of Economic Stabilization and as secretary of the Treasury. This made Vinson one of the few people in American history to have served as a member of the legislative, executive, and judicial branches of the federal government.

However, his greatest honor was to come. Truman became president in 1945 after the death of Franklin Roosevelt. Harlan Stone, the chief justice of the Supreme Court, died in 1946. Truman picked Vinson to be Stone's replacement.

Historians have mixed opinions on Vinson's term as a Supreme Court justice. Most of them are not sure how he would have voted in *Brown v. Board of Education*. Some point out that Vinson believed in a strong central government. He was still close to Truman, who had taken steps to improve civil rights throughout America during his time in office. Vinson also had supported the decision in *Sweatt v. Painter* to allow African Americans to attend an all-white law school in Texas.

On the other hand, the chief justice wondered if the Constitution could justify such a sweeping change as desegregating all public schools. Vinson also had doubts that the Supreme Court's decision could be enforced.

After Vinson died on September 8, 1953, President Dwight Eisenhower appointed Earl Warren as his replacement.

The New Chief Justice

Warren was sworn in to his new job about a month after Vinson's death. He had time to study the sides of the *Brown* case. More hearings were set for December 1953. Many of the questions in the second hearing dealt with enforcement of desegregation.

It became obvious to the other justices that Warren was a strong advocate for striking down the "separate but equal" precedent and issuing a wide ruling that would end school segregation. That would mean that at least five of nine votes would be cast in Brown's favor. However, Warren believed that a simple majority would not be enough. He went to work.

Earl Warren replaced Frederick Vinson as chief justice of the US Supreme Court. His appointment played a large role in the court's final ruling on the *Brown* case.

The chief justice assigned himself the task of writing the opinion explaining the court's decision. Then he went about the business of building a consensus on the issue. His first action was to split the case into two parts. The first part was to decide whether school segregation should be outlawed because of the Constitution. The second part was how to go about enforcing desegregation. It was a wise move under the circumstances because it gave the court more time to consider its actions.

Warren first tried to persuade Jackson. Jackson shared some of Frankfurter's concerns about a judicial ruling having such a huge effect on the country. Jackson believed that "policy decisions by the least democratic and the least representative of our branches of government are hard to justify." In other words, Jackson believed elected state officials should be responsible for making such a big policy change, not the Supreme Court.

Despite his concerns, Justice Reed went along with the rest of the Supreme Court in the *Brown* vote.

Next, Warren tried to persuade Clark. He had frequently followed Vinson's lead when it came to votes. However, Clark wandered a bit between liberal and conservative viewpoints. He grew up in Texas. He was scared of what might happen in the South if school desegregation was immediately installed. Nevertheless, he was on Warren's side.

That left Reed as the one potential holdout to a unanimous decision. Reed knew he had no chance at victory. Reed started to write a dissent to the decision. However, he realized that going against the majority would only add to potential uproar in the South. After a discussion with Warren, Reed agreed to vote with the majority.

The Court Announces Its Decision

Only a few people knew what was coming on May 17, 1954, when the decision would be announced in public. Maybe they received a hint when Jackson showed up to sit in his chair. He had been hospitalized for almost two months beforehand.

The Supreme Court justices who ruled on *Brown v. Board of Education* in 1954: (*clockwise from top left*) Clark, Jackson, Burton, Minton, Douglas, Reed, Warren, Black, and Frankfurter

Earl Warren

Earl Warren is one of the most important Supreme Court justices in American history. Associate Justice Abe Fortas once said Warren led "the most profound and pervasive revolution ever achieved by substantially peaceful means." In other words, Warren was capable for peacefully making great changes.

Warren grew up in California and was a district attorney in Alameda County for eighteen years. He was elected California's attorney general in 1938 and the state's governor in 1942. A two-time contender to be the Republican nominee for president, Warren put aside his own presidential ambitions and supported Dwight Eisenhower's candidacy in 1952. When Eisenhower won, Warren received a reward of sorts when he was nominated to be the US Supreme Court's chief justice in 1953. The *Brown v. Board of Education* case was waiting when he got to the Supreme Court. He helped navigate the court to a unanimous decision.

Warren became a strong advocate of individual rights. He had a strong sense of justice and common sense throughout his time on the Supreme Court. Warren believed the courts should be an active part of government. After his retirement in 1969, followers and critics both agreed that his impact on America was enormous.

However, the associate justice wanted to personally show that the court was unified in its decision. He checked out of the hospital, against his doctor's orders, to attend.

At 12:52 p.m., Warren began to read his relatively brief opinion. For several minutes, it was impossible to tell what the court's ruling was. During the next twenty-eight minutes, Warren's words grew in intensity.

Warren's opinion pointed out that "separate but equal" did not emerge until 1896. He pointed out that it was a case involving transportation and not education. Warren went on to state that segregation in our schools meant African Americans did not have the "equal protection" guaranteed by the Fourteenth Amendment. He wrote:

> Today [education] is a principal instrument in awakening the child to cultural values, in preparing him for later professional training, and in helping him to adjust normally to his environment. In these days, it is doubtful that any child may reasonably be expected to succeed in life if he is denied the opportunity of an education. Such an opportunity, where the state has undertaken to provide it, is a right which must be made available to all on equal terms.

Warren then directly quoted the lower court's original opinion in the *Brown* case, which acknowledged the negative emotional effects of segregation, even as it upheld the policy:

> "Segregation of white and colored children in public schools has a detrimental effect upon the colored children. The impact is greater when it has the sanction of the law, for the policy of separating the

> races is usually interpreted as denoting the inferiority of the Negro group.["] ... Any language in *Plessy v. Ferguson* contrary to this finding is rejected. We conclude that, in the field of public education, the doctrine of "separate but equal" has no place. Separate educational facilities are inherently unequal.

In other words, Warren understood that education was necessary for all people to succeed in life. He also understood that separate education facilities had a negative effect on African American children. The court ruled that these separate facilities were unconstitutional.

Brown v. Board of Education of Topeka (2)

The road to school desegregation was a long, difficult struggle. Many thought it would never take place. However, after the *Brown* decision, segregated schools were illegal across the country. Unfortunately, the court ruling was just the first step.

The Decision

Does the segregation of public education based solely on race violate the equal protection clause of the Fourteenth Amendment?

Yes: Warren, Black, Burton, Clark, Douglas, Frankfurter, Jackson, Minton, Reed

Despite the victory, big questions still remained. These questions involved who would take responsibility for changing the school systems and how fast could it be done. Northern states desegregated their schools with little problem. Border states generally did the same. The process went quite smoothly in Topeka, Kansas. In fact, the Topeka Board of Education voted to ended school segregation in the district in September 1953, in the midst of the Supreme Court battle. In 1954, Linda Brown was attending an integrated junior high school.

However, in the South, there was resistance to desegregation. The Supreme Court justices debated the issue in April 1955 without Jackson, who died the previous year. John Marshall Harlan II, the grandson of the one justice who was against the *Plessy v. Ferguson* decision, replaced Jackson. However, the justices did not want to become "the nation's school board." In *Brown v. Board of Education (2)*, the justices decided to leave it up to lower courts to make sure cities and towns followed the new rules. In their May 1955 ruling, the court unanimously told the nation to end segregation. "Racial discrimination in public education is unconstitutional, and all provisions of federal, state or local law requiring or permitting such discrimination must yield to this principle," the court ordered. In other words, all public institutions were forced to desegregate.

However, there was a huge loophole, or a way for people to not comply. The decision ordered that changes in the education system be made "with all deliberate speed." What did that mean? Did it order schools to desegregate as soon as possible, perhaps as quickly as the next school year?

No one was sure.

FIVE

A Variety of Consequences

It did not take long for political leaders to react to the *Brown v. Board of Education* decision. Statements often followed racial and geographic lines.

Writers for the *Chicago Defender*, a leading African American newspaper, believed that "neither the atom bomb nor the hydrogen bomb will ever be as meaningful to our

Some schools were quick to integrate classrooms, but others were defiant.

democracy as the unanimous declaration of the Supreme Court that racial segregation violates the spirit and the letter of our Constitution." In other words, the decision dramatically changed the course of history.

Robert Jackson, a professor of black history at Virginia Union University, said:

> I haven't seen such collective emotion since the day [Franklin] Roosevelt died. A lot of us haven't been breathing for the past nine months. But today the students reacted as if a heavy burden had been lifted from their shoulders. They see a new world opening up for them and those that follow them.

He believed many African Americans felt like they could breathe for the first time in months. The decision lifted a weight and opened new doors of opportunity for them to walk through.

Senator James Eastland urged schools to ignore the ruling.

There were certainly different feelings about the decision among white Southerners. Senator James Eastland of Mississippi declared that "the South will not abide by nor obey this legislative decision by a political body." In other words, the Southern states were not going to obey the court's ruling.

Similarly, Senator Harry Byrd of Virginia called the decision "the most serious blow that has yet been struck against the rights of the states." Byrd wanted a law passed that would take away the state funding of any school that integrated. If the school remained opened after that, the law would close it.

The Immediate Aftermath

One of the first battlegrounds was located in Tennessee. Clinton High School in Anderson County did not have any black students. African Americans were bused out of the county to Knoxville to attend school. That prompted a lawsuit, which was being appealed when the *Brown* decision reached the Supreme Court.

Riots broke out at a high school in Clinton, Tennessee, in response to desegregation. The National Guard was called in to restore order.

A local judge ordered the high school to accept black students in the fall of 1956. Twelve African Americans registered for school at Clinton. Their first day went without incident. However, a white segregationist named John Kasper came to the town of Clinton in an attempt to lead protests and to threaten violent actions. A judge ordered Kasper's arrest, and a riot broke out. Frank Clement was Tennessee's governor at the time. He had been elected as a segregationist but decided to follow the *Brown* decision. He ordered one hundred patrolmen and six hundred National Guard soldiers to restore order, and they did.

Clinton's problems were not over. People shot at several African American families. A priest who escorted black students to school was severely beaten. In the spring of 1957, Clinton student Bobby Cain became the first African American to graduate from an integrated public high school in the South. In 1958, the school itself was blown up with seventy-six sticks of dynamite on a Sunday morning. No arrests were made. The entire community, black and white, worked together to repair an abandoned school that served as a temporary home for the students.

A similar situation unfolded in Little Rock, Arkansas. On September 2, 1957, Governor Orval Faubus called in the National Guard to surround Little Rock Central High School. He ordered the soldiers to prevent black students from entering the school. Faubus claimed he was just trying to "preserve the peace." At the time, he was worried about being reelected. The National Guard continued that job until ordered to leave by a federal judge on September 20.

Three days later, protesters and Little Rock police officers circled the high school. Nine African Americans were

African American students like Elizabeth Eckford had to face protesters and demonstrations like the one pictured here on their first days at Little Rock Central High School in Arkansas.

enrolling in Little Rock Central. The police were there to help the students. The officers slipped the students in through a side door. When word spread, the crowd became angry, and the students left the school before noon. A day later, government officials asked President Dwight Eisenhower for help. The 101st Airborne Division of the US Army was sent to Little Rock to assist.

The next day, those troops allowed the nine students to enter the front door of Little Rock Central. White mobs taunted the students as they went into the building. They also injured black reporters covering the story. The events were documented on film, and the violence was shown on television news programs throughout the country. It gave Americans the chance to see what was actually happening.

Similar media coverage and pictures would have a huge impact on civil rights attitudes during the next twelve years. The United States Army remained on duty at Little Rock Central for the rest of the school year.

Virginia had a statewide response to the *Brown* decision. Senator Byrd called for "Massive Resistance" to the desegregation order. State officials followed that lead by taking several steps to prevent enforcement of the court decision. Governor Thomas Stanley threatened to close any school that had been ordered to desegregate. The state tried to restrict the NAACP's ability to file lawsuits on such cases. Additionally, some state officials worked to convince the public not to follow the court orders.

By 1958, the courts had ordered the schools to integrate immediately. Virginia officials responded by closing schools. This set up a series of legal battles. Eventually, most school districts integrated their schools. However, Prince Edward County chose to close its schools rather than open them to African Americans. It took until 1964—five years after the county's schools were closed—for the Supreme Court to reopen them. The legal battles continued until 1968.

The battle over segregation in education in the South extended to universities. In September 1962, James Meredith, an African American, attempted to enroll at the University of Mississippi. Riots broke out. Two people were killed and hundreds were injured. Meredith graduated a year later. In Alabama in 1963, Vivian Malone and James A. Hood tried to register at that state's university. Governor George Wallace literally stood in the doorway of the school to prevent the African Americans from enrolling. President John F. Kennedy ordered one hundred Alabama National Guard soldiers to

James Meredith faced violent protests when he registered for classes at the University of Mississippi. He both enrolled in and graduated from the institution.

help Malone and Hood register. Wallace eventually moved out of the way.

Bit by bit, the forces for integration prevailed. The Civil Rights Act of 1964 was a huge step in that direction. There were several court cases that helped as well. For instance, in *Green v. County School Board of New Kent County* (1968), a town in Virginia offered students the chance to choose which of two schools they wanted to attend. They could choose the one that had been all-black or the one that had been all-white. In the US Supreme Court's 1968 ruling in the case, the court decided that "freedom of choice" was not an acceptable method for attempting to desegregate those schools. It ordered school districts to dismantle segregated schools "root and branch." A year later, the court threw out its standard of integrating schools with "all deliberate speed." It ordered schools to desegregate immediately.

Then, in 1971, *Swann v. Charlotte-Mecklenburg Board of Education* took on the matter of busing. In the mid-1960s, less than 5 percent of African American students were attending integrated schools in Charlotte, North Carolina. A federal district court ordered that buses be used as a tool to integrate schools in that city. In other words, students would be bused to schools in different areas of the city in order to create more racially diverse student bodies. The Supreme Court agreed with this approach.

The Long-Term Effects

The story doesn't end there, naturally. The battle over the makeup of our schools has continued in one form or another ever since the *Brown v. Board of Education* decision. As of 2016, about 84 percent of all African Americans held a high school diploma. While that was relatively close to the 89 percent of white Americans who had graduated high school, a racial disparity remained. About 20 percent of African Americans held a college degree, versus 32 percent of white Americans. The number of African American college graduates before the *Brown* decision was about 2.5 percent. Additionally, the gap in reading scores between white and black Americans has shrunk since 1954.

Although there have been many positive results, a perfect solution remains difficult to achieve. Several courts across the country ordered busing in large cities to enforce desegregation. This led to some huge conflicts in many cases. Boston is one of the most famous stories. The courts asked that individual schools reflect the racial makeup of the whole

History's Viewpoints

The case of *Brown v. Board of Education of Topeka* was a landmark decision for racial relations. People still weigh in on how effective the decision was in reaching the goal of racial equality in education.

"The existence of racial disparities throughout education systems in this country sets forth the challenges we face," said Leticia Smith-Evans of the NAACP in 2014. "This should serve as a call to action, one that requires us to move forward swiftly to address the barriers that students, particularly those of color, face." In other words, Smith believes we still have a long way to go.

Even though the *Brown* decision did not fix all race-related issues in education, it was a necessary first step. "When you look at *Brown* you are looking at a moment so powerful it is the equivalent of the Big Bang in our solar system," historian Juan Williams argues. "It led to the Civil Rights Act of 1964 and the Voting Rights Act of 1965. It led to sit-ins and bus rides and freedom marches. And even today ... the power of *Brown* continues to stir the nation." In other words, despite some continued bumps in the road, *Brown v. Board of Education of Topeka* changed this country forever.

district, rather than the makeup of individual neighborhoods. School attendance dropped and people protested in response. Some of these protests turned violent.

Additionally, school desegregation certainly has been a factor in the changing racial makeup of cities. Many white families moved to the suburbs during the years after the *Brown* case. There were a number of reasons for that. The result has been that suburban school districts are mostly white, while minorities make up the majority of students in cities.

In recent years, studies have shown that metropolitan areas have become more diverse overall. However, people still tend to live around others that share the same racial backgrounds. In other words, white people live in neighborhoods generally surrounded by white people. The same is true for black people and black neighborhoods. For these reasons, some schools tend to have a high majority from one racial background.

In 1988, school integration reached an all-time high. Forty-five percent of black students were attending schools with a majority of white students. However, the numbers have dropped since then because court decisions have allowed communities to have more control over the racial makeup of their schools.

In March 2018, Linda Brown, whose family fought to end segregation, died at age seventy-five. Her legacy, however, will continue to live on. Although the dream that America's children will be educated together continues to prove difficult to fully achieve, *Brown v. Board of Education of Topeka* remains responsible for much of the success of integration over the past several decades. The bravery of the Brown family will certainly be remembered by those who continue to fight for equality.

Chronology

1857 The Supreme Court rules that African Americans are not American citizen and, therefore, have no right to sue (*Dred Scott v. Sandford*).

1868 The Fourteenth Amendment to the United States Constitution is ratified, or made official. One part of it reads that no state can "deny to any person within its jurisdiction the equal protection of the laws."

1875 The Civil Rights Act of 1875, designed to protect all citizens' rights to fair treatment in public accommodations and transportation, is signed into law by President Ulysses S. Grant.

1883 The Supreme Court rules that the Civil Rights Act of 1875 is unconstitutional (*Civil Rights Cases*).

1896 The Supreme Court rules that having separate but equal railroad cars for white and black passengers does not violate the Fourteenth Amendment (*Plessy v. Ferguson*).

1950 The Supreme Court rules that an African American law student must be allowed to enter the all-white University of Texas, since the state law school for African Americans was clearly not equal to the one used by white Americans (*Sweatt v. Painter*).

1951 Leola and Oliver Brown join a lawsuit against segregated schools in Topeka, Kansas.

1952 Arguments take place before the Supreme Court in what came to be known as *Brown v. Board of Education of Topeka*.

1953 Earl Warren is named chief justice of the Supreme Court after the death of Frederick Vinson. Further arguments are heard in the *Brown* case.

1954 The Supreme Court rules that school segregation is illegal (*Brown v. Board of Education of Topeka*).

1955 The Supreme Court rules that educational systems must desegregate "with all deliberate speed" (*Brown v. Board of Education of Topcka 2*).

1964 The Civil Rights Act of 1964 is signed into law by President Lyndon B. Johnson. It bans discrimination on the basis of race, gender, national origin, color, and religion.

Glossary

abridge To limit or reduce.

appeal To request that a higher court reverse the decision of a lower court.

border states States that allowed slavery before the Civil War but did not leave the Union to join the Confederacy. These states included Delaware, Kentucky, Maryland, and Missouri. West Virginia, which was carved out of western Virginia to become a state during the Civil War, is also considered a border state.

Cold War The name given to the competition between groups of nations, led by the United States and Soviet Union, in their efforts to influence world events. It took place between 1945 and 1990. Despite extremely high tensions and strong disagreements during that time, no direct military action between the countries took place.

colored A term previously used to describe African Americans. It is now considered offensive.

defendants The side that is accused or sued in a legal action.

discrimination Unjust treatment of a group of people, often based on race, age, or sex.

dissenting opinion A written statement by a judge who does not agree with the majority of other judges involved in the case.

filibuster In politics, an attempt to delay or stop the approval of a piece of proposed legislation. The word usually is associated with long speeches, made by one representative or a group of them taking turns.

Jim Crow A name used to describe laws and customs that enforced segregation in the South. It originated from a white entertainer named Thomas Dartmouth Rice. In the 1830s and 1840s, he darkened his face, acted in bumbling ways, and spoke in an exaggerated dialect to negatively portray African Americans. He called the character "Jim Crow."

loophole A means of escape or evasion. In the legal sense, it may allow one side to avoid following the purpose of an order or contract.

opinion A written legal explanation of the decision in a case and the reasoning for the case's outcome.

plaintiff A party that brings a case to court.

precedent An earlier action that can serve as a guide on how to decide similar cases in the future. Courts often rely on precedents when issuing decisions on legal cases.

public accommodations Any facility used by the public, including retail stores, lodging, recreational centers, etc.

Reconstruction The era from 1865 to 1877 in which the North tried to transform the laws and culture of the South after the Civil War. Federal troops were stationed in the South in that era to enforce those changes. Three amendments to the Constitution were passed during that time, including one that abolished slavery.

segregated Separated or divided, often by race.

seniority A ranking of members of a group based on the length of time that they were a part of that group. In Congress, representatives who have served the longest (who have seniority) usually are chosen to head committees.

solicitor general The person who supervises and conducts government legal actions in the US Supreme Court.

test case A legal action designed to set a precedent. An example is when a person or group files a lawsuit in an attempt to see if a particular situation applies to a current law.

testimony A sworn legal written or spoken statement, often made in a court of law.

Further Information

Books

Bell, Derrick. *Silent Covenants: Brown v Board of Education and the Unfulfilled Hopes for Racial Reform*. New York: Oxford University Press, 2004.

Patterson, James T. *Brown v. Board of Education: A Civil Rights Milestone and Its Troubled Legacy.* New York: Oxford University Press, 2001.

Rubin, Susan Goldman. *Brown v. Board of Education: A Fight for Simple Justice*. New York: Holiday House Books, 2016.

Telgen, Diane. *Defining Moments: Brown v. Board of Education*. Detroit: Omnigraphics, 2005.

Websites

Brown v. Board at Fifty: "With an Even Hand"

https://www.loc.gov/exhibits/brown/brown-brown.html

This website provides background on the *Brown v. Board of Education* decision.

"How *Brown v. Board of Education* Changed—and Didn't Change—American Education"

https://www.theatlantic.com/education/archive/2014/04/two-milestones-in-education/361222/

This article by Ronald Brownstein discusses the long-term effects of *Brown v. Board.*

Separate is Not Equal

http://americanhistory.si.edu/brown/history

This website for the Smithsonian's National Museum of American History gives a detailed history of the background of the case.

Videos

Brown v. Board Documentary

https://www.youtube.com/watch?v=jLcac0KIQHo

This PBS documentary gives a detailed history of segregated schools, the *Brown* case, and the case's aftermath.

Brown v. Board of Education (1954): Separate Is NOT Equal

https://www.youtube.com/watch?v=aX9Dmo24_cc&t

This video gives a quick overview of the *Brown v. Board of Education* case.

Thurgood Marshall (History for Kids)

https://www.youtube.com/watch?v=9UtxSIXr5yM&t=36s

This video discusses the life and legacy of Thurgood Marshall.

Selected Bibliography

"Beginnings of Black Education." Virginia Historical Society. Accessed November 16, 2017. http://www.vahistorical.org/collections-and-resources/virginia-history-explorer/civil-rights-movement-virginia/beginnings-black.

Bell, Debra. "George Wallace Stood in a Doorway at the University of Alabama 50 Years Ago Today." *US News & World Report*, June 11, 2013. https://www.usnews.com/news/blogs/press-past/2013/06/11/george-wallace-stood-in-a-doorway-at-the-university-of-alabama-50-years-ago-today.

"Bitter Resistance: Clarendon County, South Carolina." Smithsonian. Accessed November 10, 2017. http://americanhistory.si.edu/brown/history/4-five/clarendon-county-1.html.

"A Brief History of Jim Crow." Constitutional Rights Foundation. Accessed November 9, 2017. http://www.crf-usa.org/black-history-month/a-brief-history-of-jim-crow.

"Brown v. Board of Education Timeline." National Archives. Accessed December 13, 2017. https://www.archives.gov/education/lessons/brown-v-board/timeline.html.

"Dred Scott's Fight for Freedom." PBS. Accessed November 9, 2017. http://www.pbs.org/wgbh/aia/part4/4p2932.html.

"Earl Warren Biography." Street Law. Accessed November 15, 2017. http://landmarkcases.org/en/Page/523/Earl_Warren_biography.

"Fred M. Vinson, Jr." Oyez. Accessed November 14, 2017. https://www.oyez.org/justices/fred_m_vinson.

"The History Behind the Little Rock Nine." Arkansas Department of Parks and Tourism. Accessed November 15, 2017. https://www.arkansas.com/attractions/central-high.

Kluger, Richard. *Simple Justice: The History of* Brown v. Board of Education *and Black America's Struggle for Equality.* New York: Knopf, 2004.

Magnusson, Marcus. "No Rights Which the White Man Was Bound to Respect." American Constitution Society. March 19, 2007. https://www.acslaw.org/acsblog/no-rights-which-the-white-man-was-bound-to-respect.

Mansfield, Duncan. "A Tennessee Town Marks Desegregation Clinton Schools Integrated 50 Years Ago." *Washington Post*, October 15, 2006. https://www.washingtonpost.com/archive/politics/2006/10/15/a-tennessee-town-marks-desegregation-span-classbankheadclinton-schools-integrated-50-years-agospan/1ec30402-a152-4d68-9113-135397fbfc6c/?utm_term=.36c0909a2a56.

Menaker, Richard G. "FDR's Court-Packing Plan: A Study in Irony." Gilder Lehrman Institute of American History. Accessed November 13, 2017. https://www.gilderlehrman.org/history-by-era/new-deal/essays/fdr%E2%80%99s-court-packing-plan-study-irony.

"*Missouri ex rel. Gaines v. Canada*." Oyez. Accessed November 13, 2017. https://www.oyez.org/cases/1900-1940/305us337.

"*Plessy v. Ferguson* Court Case Facts." Black History Facts. Accessed November 9, 2017. http://www.black-history-facts.com/Black-History-Facts-Important-Court-Cases/Plessy-vs-Ferguson-Court-Case-Facts.html.

Index

About the Author

Budd Bailey retired as an editor and reporter for the *Buffalo News* in 2017. Before starting at the newspaper in 1993, he also worked for WEBR Radio. Bailey currently works as a freelance writer. He has written several books for Cavendish Square, including biographies of Booker T. Washington and Jackie Robinson. Bailey and his wife, Jody, live in Buffalo, New York.